Veg Out

Veg Out

60 knockout recipes for the laid-back cook

MQP

Published by **MQ Publications Limited**
12 The Ivories
6–8 Northampton Street
London N1 2HY
Tel: +44 (0)20 7359 2244
Fax: +44 (0)20 7359 1616
email: mail@mqpublications.com
website: www.mqpublications.com

DESIGN: **Balley Design Associates**
EDITOR: **Leanne Bryan**
PHOTOGRAPHY: **Russell Capps**

ISBN: 1-84072-508-7

10 9 8 7 6 5 4 3 2 1

Printed and bound in France

Introduction

Put your finger on the pulse of contemporary vegetarian cooking and bring flavor, beauty, and excitement to your plate with this irresistible feast of creative meat-free dishes.

Veg Out is an impressive collection of delicious and innovative recipes spanning all levels of cooking ability from novice to master. Using the best of fresh, healthy ingredients you can build depth and flavor into a tempting range of vegetable dishes.

So brush the cobwebs off your potato peeler and venture into your vegetable cupboard! Enjoy the velvety, rich texture of Cream of Butternut Squash and Coconut Soup; appreciate the elegant spectacle of the Pear and Roquefort Salad; savor the gutsy flavor of our Red Pesto and Ricotta Stacks; relish the nutty bite of the Quattro Formaggi Pizza with Walnuts; and experience the aromatic fragrance of our Pumpkin Couscous.

Searching for a hip new salad to liven up a summer barbeque? Check out our Glorious Greens. Need a comforting soup for a cold winter evening? Look no further than Stir It Up. Cooking dinner for a vegetarian friend? Go straight to The Main Event!

Cook up a culinary storm—Veg Out!

1

Stir It Up
Lip-smacking flavorful soups

Spring Vegetable Soup

A deliciously light vegetable soup using the best spring ingredients. Try to use a good homemade vegetable stock for the best flavor.

SERVES 4–6

2 tbsp sunflower oil
2 leeks, cut into ½in/1cm slices
2 stalks celery, cut into ½in/1cm slices
12 asparagus tips, coarsely chopped
8 new potatoes, cut into bite-size pieces
5 cups/1.2 liters vegetable stock
1¼ cups/150g shelled fresh peas
3 tbsp chopped fresh mint
2oz/50g baby spinach leaves
Salt and freshly ground black pepper

1 Heat the oil in a saucepan, add the leeks and celery, and cook gently, 10 minutes. Don't let the leeks brown too much or they'll taste bitter.

2 Add the asparagus and potatoes to the pan with the stock. Bring to a boil, then turn the heat down, and simmer, 15 minutes. Add the peas and simmer an additional 5 minutes.

3 Stir the mint into the soup with the baby spinach leaves. Taste and season, then serve immediately.

French Onion Soup

A good, full-flavored, rich stock is an essential prerequisite to the success of this classic French soup.

SERVES 4

2 tbsp olive oil
1 tbsp/15g butter
2 bay leaves
1lb/450g onions, sliced
5 cups/1.2 liters vegetable stock
12 thick slices French bread
1 cup/120g grated Gruyère cheese
2 tbsp dry sherry
Salt and freshly ground black pepper

1 Heat the oil and butter in a large saucepan. Add the bay leaves and onions. Stir well to coat the onions in the oil and butter, then cook over a very low heat, stirring occasionally, until the onions have browned, 20–30 minutes.

2 Add the stock and a little seasoning. Bring to a boil, reduce the heat, and cover the pan. Simmer gently, about 30 minutes.

3 Just before the soup is ready, preheat the broiler (grill). Toast the bread on one side. Top the untoasted side with the cheese and broil until melted, bubbling, and golden. Stir the sherry into the soup, taste for seasoning, and ladle into warmed bowls. Add three slices of toasted cheese bread to each portion and serve immediately.

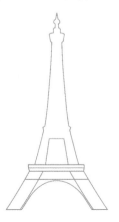

Cream of Wild Mushroom Soup

This is a luscious soup—the compliments will all be flowing in your direction. Just nod serenely, and don't mention how ridiculously easy it is to make.

SERVES 4

4 tbsp/55g butter
1 onion, finely chopped
1 garlic clove, finely chopped
1lb/450g mixed wild mushrooms, such as girolles, chanterelles, and morels
2oz/50g white bread, crusts removed
3 tbsp dry sherry
5 cups/1.2 liters vegetable stock
1 cup/250ml milk
1 tbsp chopped fresh thyme
½ cup/125ml heavy (double) cream
Salt and freshly ground black pepper
1 tbsp chopped fresh parsley, to garnish
Bread croûtons, to serve

1 Melt the butter in a large saucepan, add the onion and garlic, and cook, 10 minutes. Add the mushrooms and cook for another 10 minutes.

2 Soak the bread for a few seconds in a little water, squeeze out, and add to the saucepan with the sherry, stock, milk, and thyme. Bring to a boil, then turn the heat down, and simmer, 20 minutes. Let cool a little, then stir in the cream.

3 Puree the soup in a blender until very smooth. Taste, and season with salt and pepper. Just before serving, stir in the parsley and scatter with the croûtons.

Vichyssoise

This classic leek and potato soup is simple to make and tastes equally delicious whether served hot or cold.

SERVES 4

2 tbsp/25g butter
1 onion, chopped
1 bay leaf
1lb/450g leeks, sliced
2 potatoes, diced
2½ cups/600ml vegetable stock
1 cup/250ml milk
⅔ cup/150ml light (single) cream
Salt and freshly ground black pepper

1 Melt the butter in a large saucepan. Add the onion and bay leaf, then stir well, and cook, 5 minutes. Add the leeks and salt and pepper to taste, then stir well again. Cover the pan and cook, stirring occasionally, until the leeks have reduced and softened, about 15 minutes.

2 Stir in the potatoes, stock, and milk. Bring to a boil and reduce the heat. Cover and simmer, 30 minutes. Cool slightly, then puree the soup until smooth in a blender or food processor.

3 To serve the soup hot, return it to the pan and reheat gently. Taste and adjust the seasoning, then stir in the cream and heat for a few seconds without boiling. Serve at once. To serve the soup chilled, let it cool, then chill for several hours. Stir in the cream and taste for seasoning before serving.

Cream of Butternut Squash & Coconut Soup

This soup has the most wonderful velvety texture and is extremely rich and filling. You can experiment with different kinds of squash depending on personal preference and market availability.

SERVES 4

2 tbsp sunflower oil
2lb/900g butternut squash, peeled, seeded, and coarsely chopped
1 onion, coarsely chopped
1 red chile, seeded and coarsely chopped
4 cups/1 liter vegetable stock
1¾ cups/450ml coconut milk
Small bunch fresh cilantro (coriander), finely chopped
Heavy (double) cream, to serve
Sprig of cilantro, to garnish.

1 Heat the oil in a fairly large saucepan and add the squash, onion, and chile. Cook, stirring, until the onion softens, 5–10 minutes.

2 Pour in the stock and simmer until the vegetables are tender, 20 minutes. Stir in the coconut milk. Let cool slightly, then puree in a blender or food processor. Stir in the cilantro and swirl the cream on top of the soup just before serving. Garnish with a sprig of cilantro.

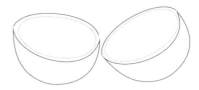

Ribollita

More of a vegetable stew than a soup, Ribollita is a hearty Italian dish, perfect for lunch on a cold winter's day. Cavolo nero is the authentic vegetable to use, but cabbage or Swiss chard are acceptable substitutes.

SERVES 4–6

5 tbsp olive oil
3 stalks celery, coarsely chopped
4 carrots, coarsely chopped
2 red onions, coarsely chopped
3 garlic cloves, finely chopped
7oz/200g can chopped tomatoes
5 cups/1.2 liters vegetable stock
2 large handfuls cavolo nero, cabbage, or Swiss chard, coarsely chopped
11oz/300g canned borlotti or cannellini beans, drained
Small ciabatta loaf, about 6oz/175g
Salt and freshly ground black pepper
Extra-virgin olive oil, to serve

1 Heat the oil in a large saucepan. Add the fresh vegetables and garlic and cook gently, 25–30 minutes. Stir occasionally to prevent the vegetables from burning.

2 Add the tomatoes and stock and simmer, 15 minutes. Add the cavolo nero, cabbage or Swiss chard to the pan with half the beans. Season well and simmer an additional 20 minutes.

3 Mash or puree the remaining beans. Cut the bread into small cubes. Stir both the beans and the bread into the soup and add a splash of extra-virgin olive oil just before serving.

Glorious Green Soup

This summer soup really has the most glorious full-of-goodness flavor. Serve it piping hot or ice cold.

SERVES 4

2 tbsp olive oil
1 onion, coarsely chopped
3 potatoes, cut into chunks
2½ cups/600ml vegetable stock
1 Romaine or Cos lettuce heart, coarsely shredded
1 bunch watercress, about 3½oz/ 90g, trimmed
1¼ cups/300ml milk
Handful fresh basil sprigs, shredded
Handful fresh mint sprigs, chopped
Salt and freshly ground black pepper

1 Heat the oil in a large saucepan. Add the onion and cook 5 minutes, then stir in the potatoes and cook 2 minutes. Pour in the stock and bring to a boil. Reduce the heat, cover the pan, and simmer until the potatoes are very soft, 20 minutes.

2 Add the lettuce and watercress. Bring back to a boil, stirring, then reduce the heat, and cover the pan. Simmer 5 minutes. Do not worry if the soup seems very thick at this stage.

3 Cool the soup slightly before pureeing it in a blender until smooth. Return to the pan and stir in the milk. Add seasoning to taste and heat through. Stir in the basil and mint and serve immediately.

Ginger-spiced Carrot & Garbanzo Soup

This is easy to make and warming—just the recipe for a quick Saturday lunch or midweek supper in the middle of winter.

SERVES 4

2 tbsp/25g butter
1 large onion, chopped
2 tbsp freshly grated ginger
2 garlic cloves, crushed
1 bay leaf
8oz/225g carrots, sliced
2½ cups/600ml vegetable stock
14oz/400g can garbanzos
   (chickpeas), drained
1¼ cups/300ml milk
Salt and freshly ground black pepper
2 tbsp chopped fresh cilantro (coriander)
   or parsley, to garnish

1 Melt the butter in a large saucepan. Add the onion, ginger, garlic, and bay leaf. Stir well, cover, and cook, stirring occasionally, until the onion is soft but not browned, 10 minutes. Add the carrots, stock, garbanzos, and seasoning to taste. Bring to a boil, reduce the heat, and cover the pan. Simmer 30 minutes.

2 Puree the soup until smooth in a blender or food processor. Return the soup to the pan and stir in the milk. Reheat and taste for seasoning before serving, sprinkled with cilantro or parsley.

Gazpacho

This wonderful cold soup originates from the Spanish region of Andalusia. It is ideal to serve on a hot summer's day.

SERVES 4

2 red bell peppers, seeded and finely diced
1 green bell pepper, seeded and
  finely diced
½ cucumber, peeled, seeded, and
  finely diced
2 green (spring) onions, finely chopped
2 garlic cloves, finely chopped
2oz/50g slightly stale ciabatta or rustic
  bread (about 2 slices), coarsely cubed
5 cups/1.2 liters fresh tomato juice
2 tbsp white wine or sherry vinegar
3 tbsp olive oil
6 ice cubes
Fresh basil leaves, to garnish
Toasted croûtons, to serve (optional)

1 Place about two-thirds of the red and green bell peppers in a large mixing bowl and reserve the rest as a garnish.

2 Place two-thirds of the cucumber in the bowl with the bell peppers and reserve the rest for garnish. Add the green onions and garlic to the mixing bowl.

3 Place the bread in the mixing bowl. Pour the tomato juice and vinegar over the ingredients and add the olive oil. Mix and season well.

4 Using a blender or food processor, puree the soup in batches until smooth. Pour back into the bowl, add the ice cubes, and chill, at least 1 hour. Stir in the reserved diced vegetables and top with basil and croûtons, if desired.

2

Glorious Greens

Salads to satisfy the soul

Roasted Beet Salad
with oranges & goat cheese

Use fresh beets (beetroots) to bring out
the full flavor of this salad—although
canned, precooked beets can be used as a
substitute. Use whichever kind of goat
cheese you like best—sharp French
chèvre is a good one.

SERVES 4

6 fresh beets (beetroots), washed
2 oranges, peeled and segmented
5oz/150g goat cheese
1 tbsp chopped fresh chives
Dressing
1 tbsp balsamic vinegar
1 tsp honey
4 tbsp olive oil

1 Preheat the oven to 350°F/180°C,
Gas 4. Pierce the beets with a skewer or
point of a sharp knife and place in a
roasting pan. Roast until tender, 1½ hours.
Cool, then peel off the skins. Cut into
½in/1cm thick wedges and place in a
serving bowl.

2 To make the dressing, mix the vinegar,
honey, and oil together and pour it over
the roasted beets.

3 Add the oranges to the beets and
crumble the goat cheese on top. Scatter
with chives before serving.

Spiced Cucumber Tabbouleh

This lightly spiced salad of cucumber
and bulgur wheat has a fresh flavor
balanced by the unmistakable warmth of
roasted cumin seeds.

SERVES 4

1⅓ cups/225g bulgur wheat
2 tbsp cumin seeds
1 large cucumber, peeled, seeded,
  and diced
1 small green bell pepper, seeded and
  finely chopped
6 green (spring) onions, finely chopped
3 tbsp chopped fresh parsley
3 garlic cloves, finely chopped
1 tsp sugar
Juice of ½ lemon
¼ cup/60ml extra-virgin olive oil
Salt and freshly ground black pepper
Sprig of cilantro (coriander), to garnish

1 Place the bulgur wheat in a bowl and
cover with plenty of cold water. Cover and
let soak, 30 minutes. Drain in a strainer
and let stand over a bowl to drain
thoroughly, about 15 minutes.

2 Roast the cumin seeds in a small,
heavy-based saucepan over medium heat,
shaking the pan frequently until the seeds
smell aromatic. Immediately remove the
pan from the heat and turn the seeds into
a bowl. Add the cucumber, bell pepper,
green onions, chopped parsley, and garlic
to the cumin.

3 Stir in the bulgur wheat, sugar, and
lemon juice, and season with salt and
pepper to taste. Mix well so that the
seasoning and sugar dissolve in the juices.
Stir in the olive oil, cover, and chill at least
1 hour before serving. Remove the
tabbouleh from the refrigerator about
30 minutes before serving, so that it is
cool, but not chilled. Garnish with a
sprig of cilantro.

Pear & Roquefort Salad

Peppery arugula (rocket), honey-sweet pears, and salty Roquefort cheese combine beautifully in this salad, which would make an elegant appetizer.

SERVES 6

2 Romaine or Cos lettuce hearts
6oz/175g arugula (rocket)
6 small ripe pears
Dressing
⅓ cup/40g crumbled Roquefort cheese, plus extra to garnish
Scant 1 cup/225ml sour cream or crème fraîche
Salt and freshly ground black pepper

1 To make the dressing, blend the Roquefort cheese and sour cream or crème fraîche in a blender or food processor. Season with plenty of salt and pepper.

2 Separate the lettuce hearts into leaves. Wash and dry all the salad greens. Fan three or four lettuce leaves on each of six salad plates. Add the arugula leaves.

3 Cut the pears in half and carefully scoop out the cores with a teaspoon. Place each pear half in turn on a board, cut-side down, and make three parallel cuts from the rounded side to the stem end, so that each pear half is now cut into fourths. Divide the pear fourths among the six salad plates and arrange them over and between the lettuce leaves.

4 Drizzle each salad with the prepared dressing and garnish with crumbled cheese. Serve at once, with the extra dressing in a small pitcher.

> **Cook's Tip**
> If you do not intend to serve the salad immediately, brush the pear flesh with lemon juice to prevent discoloration.

Green Bean & Mozzarella Salad

Smooth, delicate mozzarella cheese is delicious with crisp, lightly cooked green beans in this zesty salad.

SERVES 4

12oz/350g fine green beans
12oz/350g mozzarella cheese, thinly sliced
Dressing
3 tbsp coriander seeds
Grated peel and juice of 1 large orange
1 tbsp cider vinegar
½ tsp sugar
1 tsp whole-grain mustard
1 small garlic clove, chopped
5 tbsp extra-virgin olive oil
3 tbsp chopped fresh parsley
Salt and freshly ground black pepper

1 To make the dressing, roast the coriander seeds in a small, heavy-based saucepan over medium heat. Shake the pan frequently until the seeds begin to smell aromatic and darken very slightly. Tip the coriander seeds into a mortar as soon as they are roasted—do not leave them in the pan or they may overcook, becoming dark and bitter. Use a pestle to crush the seeds coarsely.

2 In a bowl large enough to hold the beans, mix the seeds with the orange peel and juice, cider vinegar, sugar, mustard, and garlic. Season with salt and pepper. Whisk until the sugar and salt have dissolved, then whisk in the oil to make a slightly thickened dressing. Add the parsley to the mixture.

3 Cook the beans in a large pan of boiling water until crisp but not soft, 3 minutes. Drain and immediately add them to the dressing. Turn the beans in the dressing to cool them quickly. Cover and let marinate, about 1 hour, if possible, or at least until they are cold.

4 Add the mozzarella to the beans and mix the salad gently, taking care not to break up the cheese. Spoon onto individual plates and serve immediately.

Marinated Bean Curd

with white radish salad

A simple salad of radish with green (spring) onions perfectly complements the silky, custard-like texture of pan-fried bean curd in the finest of crisp coatings.

SERVES 2-4

11oz/300g packet firm bean curd
1 large white radish (mooli),
   coarsely grated
2 green (spring) onions, finely shredded
   at a slant
½ cucumber, peeled, halved, seeded,
   and grated
2 tbsp sunflower oil
6-8 tbsp cornstarch (cornflour)
Marinade
1 tsp sugar
1 tsp sesame oil
2 tsp Japanese rice vinegar
2 tbsp light soy sauce
2 tbsp sake or dry sherry
1 garlic clove, crushed
Pinch of chili flakes

1 To make the marinade, whisk the marinade ingredients together until the sugar has dissolved.

2 Cut the bean curd into 8 slices about ½in/1cm thick, and place in a shallow dish. Spoon the soy sauce mixture over the bean curd, cover, and marinate in the refrigerator, 1-2 hours. For a fuller flavor, marinate for up to 24 hours.

3 Mix the grated radish with the green onions and cucumber. Remove the bean curd from the marinade using a slotted spoon. Pour the marinade into the radish salad. Toss the radish salad well so that it is fully coated in the marinade.

4 Heat the oil in a nonstick skillet (frying pan). Place the cornstarch on a plate. Dip the bean curd slices in the cornstarch, turning them to coat each side. Add the bean curd slices to the skillet as they are coated, and cook each side 1-1½ minutes until crisp and pale golden. Transfer to plates and serve immediately with the radish salad.

Panzanella

Choose the juiciest, ripest tomatoes for this traditional Italian salad. Authentic versions call for chopped onion, but the garlic-steeped dressing in this version gives the dish enough kick.

SERVES 6–8

1 small ciabatta or rustic loaf, about
   6oz/175g, cut into cubes
1 cucumber, peeled, seeded, and
   coarsely chopped
4 ripe tomatoes, halved, and cut
   into chunks
2 tbsp capers, rinsed
Dressing
2 garlic cloves
2 tbsp red wine vinegar
8 tbsp olive oil
2 hard-cooked (boiled) eggs,
   coarsely chopped
8–10 fresh basil leaves
Salt and freshly ground black pepper

1 Preheat the oven to 400°F/200°C, Gas 6. Place the bread cubes on a baking sheet and toast in the oven, 10 minutes. Transfer to a high-sided salad bowl.

2 Add the cucumber and tomatoes to the salad bowl. Sprinkle with the capers.

3 To make the dressing, pound the garlic cloves in a mortar with a pestle. Whisk in the vinegar and oil, and season. Pour the dressing over the salad.

4 Arrange the hard-cooked eggs on top of the salad with the basil leaves. Let stand 15 minutes, then stir once before serving—you want the bread to soak up the juices and dressing but not become unappealingly soggy.

New York Potato Salad

For a good potato salad you need to pick the potato variety carefully. A mealy (floury) potato will result in a lumpy mash, so find good waxy new potatoes like **Long Whites, Charlotte, or Anya**. The same goes for the mayonnaise. If it's homemade, all the better, but a superior store-bought brand will do.

SERVES 6

18 new potatoes
3 stalks celery, finely chopped
4 green (spring) onions, finely chopped
1 small bunch fresh parsley, finely chopped
1 small bunch fresh chives, finely chopped
2 hard-cooked (boiled) eggs,
  coarsely chopped
Dressing
⅔ cup/150ml sour cream
¾ cup/185ml mayonnaise
1 tbsp lemon juice
Freshly ground black pepper

1 Cook the potatoes in boiling salted water until tender, 15–20 minutes. Remove from the saucepan and let cool, then peel off the skins. This is a little tedious, but worth the effort. Chop into bite-size pieces and transfer to a mixing bowl.

2 Mix the celery, green onions, and parsley into the potatoes. Add the chives to the rest of the ingredients.

3 Whisk the sour cream, mayonnaise, and lemon juice together, add plenty of black pepper and pour the mixture over the salad. Mix everything well. Add the eggs and carefully fold into the potato salad. Chill until ready to serve.

Hot Vegetable Salad

Choose small, perfect new potatoes and baby carrots for this colorful salad.

SERVES 4

28 small new potatoes, scrubbed
16 baby carrots, scrubbed
1¼ cups/150g shelled fresh or frozen peas
8 green (spring) onions, chopped
1–2 Romaine or Cos lettuce
hearts, shredded
Dressing
Handful fresh parsley sprigs
Handful fresh mint sprigs
Handful fresh dill sprigs
1 tsp sugar
1 tbsp whole-grain mustard
2 tbsp balsamic vinegar
5 tbsp extra-virgin olive oil
Salt and freshly ground black pepper

1 Place the potatoes in a large saucepan and pour in boiling water to cover. Add a little salt, then bring to a boil. Reduce the heat, cover, and simmer 10 minutes. Add the carrots and peas, and bring back to a boil, then reduce the heat again. Cover, and keep the vegetables just boiling another 5 minutes, until they are tender.

2 Meanwhile, place the parsley, mint, dill, and sugar in a food processor and process until finely chopped. Add the mustard, vinegar, salt, and pepper, then process again until well mixed. Then pour in the oil and process for a few seconds. Turn into a bowl and stir in the green onions.

3 Drain the vegetables and add them to the dressing, then toss well to coat them evenly. Arrange the lettuce in a large shallow dish and pile in the vegetable salad. Serve immediately.

Greek Salad

Dill is an unusual addition to this classic salad, but it marries surprisingly well with the tomatoes.

SERVES 4–6

4 tomatoes, coarsely chopped
½ cucumber, coarsely chopped
½ red onion, thinly sliced
2 tbsp chopped fresh dill
4oz/115g feta cheese, cubed
½ cup/50g pitted (stoned) black olives
2 tbsp olive oil
1 tbsp fresh lemon juice
Freshly ground black pepper

1 Mix together the tomatoes, cucumber, onion, and dill in a salad bowl. Season with pepper. Feta cheese can be very salty so leave it up to the individual diners to add salt according to their own taste.

2 Scatter the feta over the salad with the olives. Whisk the olive oil with the lemon juice and pour over the salad.

Strawberry & Watercress Salad

This salad celebrates the classic combination of strawberries and balsamic vinegar, setting them against a background of dark green, peppery watercress leaves and crisp celery. Delicious served with warm ciabatta.

SERVES 4

1 bunch watercress
2 stalks celery, sliced
1 small mild red onion, sliced into rings
2¼ cups/275g just-ripe strawberries, hulled and sliced in half
Dressing
2 tbsp balsamic vinegar
Pinch of sugar
1 tbsp very finely chopped shallot
6 tbsp extra-virgin olive oil
½ tsp drained pink peppercorns in vinegar
Salt

1 Trim off any tough stalks from the watercress, wash it well, then drain and pat the leaves dry with paper towels.

2 Mix the watercress, celery, and onion slices in a bowl. Add three-quarters of the strawberries to the bowl.

3 To make the dressing, put the balsamic vinegar in a small bowl, and add the sugar and shallot. Whisk to mix, then gradually whisk in the olive oil. Add salt to taste, then stir in the pink peppercorns.

4 Pour 2 tbsp of the dressing over the salad and toss lightly. Spoon onto salad plates, mounding the salad in the center. Arrange the remaining strawberries on top and serve at once, with the extra dressing in a small pitcher.

> **Cook's Tip**
>
> Some people are allergic to pink peppercorns, so always inform your guests that you have used them.

3

Naughty Nibbles
Irresistible snacks and appetizers

Red Pesto & Ricotta Stacks
with eggplant and tomato

A delicious and gutsy appetizer to serve with salad greens and charbroiled (grilled) ciabatta slices.

SERVES 6

2 tbsp olive oil
1 large eggplant (aubergine), cut into
   1in/2.5cm thick slices
2 beefsteak tomatoes, thickly sliced
Rocket leaves, to garnish
Red pesto
2 red bell peppers, halved and seeded
2 garlic cloves
⅓ cup/40g pine nuts
4 tbsp torn fresh basil leaves
⅔ cup/50g freshly grated Parmesan cheese
2 tbsp ricotta cheese
2 tbsp olive oil

1 Preheat the oven to 400°F/200°C, Gas 6. To make the pesto, put the bell peppers on a baking sheet, cut-side down, and place under a hot broiler (grill) until the skins are charred, 10–15 minutes.

2 Transfer the bell peppers to a plastic bag until cool, then peel off the skins. Place in a food processor with the remaining pesto ingredients and blend to a coarse paste.

3 Heat the oil in a skillet (frying pan) and brown the eggplant in batches, 2 minutes each side. Drain on paper towels.

4 Lay four of the largest eggplant slices on a nonstick baking sheet. Spread a heaped teaspoon of the pesto over each slice and top with a slice of tomato. Continue this once more ending with a slice of tomato.

5 Cook the eggplant stacks in the oven, 15 minutes. Transfer to serving plates. Garnish with rocket leaves.

> **Cook's Tip**
> A food processor blends the ingredients for the pesto sauce quickly and thoroughly, but if you've time, do it by hand in a large mortar with a pestle.

Falafel with herb & yogurt dip

These Middle Eastern patties are traditionally stuffed in pita breads filled with salad, and served with a herb dip.

SERVES 4

14oz/400g can garbanzos
  (chickpeas), drained
2 garlic cloves
1 tbsp tahini paste
2 tsp ground cumin
1 tsp ground turmeric
½ tsp cayenne pepper
2 eggs
1 small bunch fresh cilantro (coriander)
All-purpose (plain) flour, seasoned with
  salt and pepper, to taste
Oil, for deep-frying
Salad greens, to garnish

Dip
1 small bunch fresh mint, finely chopped
1 small bunch fresh parsley, finely chopped
1 small bunch fresh chives, finely chopped
1 cup/225g plain yogurt

1 Place all the ingredients for the falafel, except the flour and oil for frying, in a food processor, season, and blend until smooth.

2 Shape the mixture into patties, about 1 tbsp of mixture per patty, and roll in the seasoned flour. Heat the oil to 350°F/180°C and deep-fry the falafel until golden, 3–4 minutes. Drain on paper towels.

3 To make the dip, mix the herbs with the yogurt. Taste, and season if necessary. Serve the falafel warm with the dip on the side and garnished with salad greens, or in pita breads garnished with salad and spread with the herb dip.

Eggs Florentine

with beurre rouge

This variation of a classic French butter sauce (beurre blanc) is made with a reduction of red wine. It is delicious with poached eggs or poured over vegetables. Serve this dish with charbroiled (grilled) ciabatta bread.

SERVES 4

1 tbsp/15g butter
1 garlic clove, crushed
1½lb/675g baby leaf spinach, washed
4 extra large eggs
Sauce
6 tbsp red wine
2 shallots, finely chopped
1 tbsp sour cream or crème fraîche
1 cup/225g very cold butter, cubed
1 tsp sun-dried tomato paste
Salt and freshly ground black pepper

1 To make the red butter sauce, boil the wine and shallots in a small heavy-based saucepan until it has reduced to 1 tbsp of liquid. Add the sour cream or crème fraîche and cook until reduced a little. Whisk in the butter, a cube at a time, letting each piece melt before adding the next. Season to taste and stir in the tomato paste. Set aside.

2 Heat the butter for the spinach in a saucepan and add the garlic. Cook 1 minute, then add the spinach, cover, and let wilt, 1–2 minutes.

3 Break the eggs into a pan of boiling water and poach until the whites are firm but the yolks are still soft, 3–4 minutes. Drain the spinach and spoon onto serving plates. Top with a drained poached egg and spoon over a little tomato butter sauce. Grind some black pepper over the top before serving.

Latkes

These grated potato pancakes are popular in Jewish cooking, Scandinavian countries, and all over Eastern Europe.

MAKES ABOUT 24

1½lb/675g potatoes, peeled and coarsely grated
1 egg, beaten
3 tbsp all-purpose (plain) flour
Sunflower oil, for frying
Salt and freshly ground black pepper

1 Place the potatoes in a strainer and rinse under cold running water, then squeeze the moisture out of them. Transfer to a bowl, and add the egg with plenty of seasoning. Stir in the flour.

2 Heat a little oil in a skillet (frying pan). Stir the potato mixture, then place a spoonful in the pan, and quickly spread the grated potatoes into an evenly thick round. Repeat with more mixture, adding as many pancakes as will comfortably fit in the pan with a little space in between.

3 Cook over moderate heat until the pancakes are crisp and golden underneath. Turn and cook the other side until crisp and golden. Use a spatula to remove the pancakes from the pan, and drain individually on paper towels. Keep the pancakes hot until all the remaining mixture is cooked.

Avocado with pistachio filling

The pistachio filling adds plenty of flavor to the delicate avocado without overpowering it. Serve with crostini.

SERVES 4

4in/10cm piece cucumber, peeled and finely diced
Grated peel of ½ lime, plus extra to garnish
3 tbsp chopped fresh chives
1 cup/225g cream cheese or ricotta cheese
1 tsp pistachio oil
A little freshly grated nutmeg
Squeeze of lime juice
2 ripe avocados
2 tbsp pistachio nuts, finely chopped
Salt and freshly ground black pepper

1 Mix the cucumber with the lime peel, chives, cream cheese or ricotta, and pistachio oil. Stir until the cucumber and cheese are thoroughly combined, then season with salt, pepper, and nutmeg to taste. Add a squeeze of lime juice. Chill the mixture well.

2 When ready to serve, halve and pit the avocados. Stir the chilled filling well, then use a teaspoon to pile it into the center of the avocados. Sprinkle with pistachio nuts and and top with the lime peel. Serve immediately.

Variations

• Use 4 peeled, seeded, and diced tomatoes instead of cucumber.
• For a lighter flavor, use walnut oil and chopped walnuts instead of pistachio oil and chopped pistachio nuts.

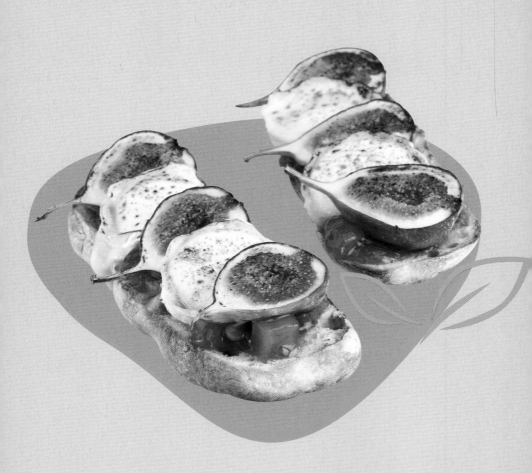

Fig & Goat Cheese Bruschetta

Serve this simple dish as a light lunch or sensational appetizer. It looks gorgeous, and the combination of melted goat cheese and warm figs with just a hint of mango chutney is irresistible.

SERVES 6

1 small ciabatta or similar loaf, about
   10in/25cm long, halved lengthwise
¼ cup/65g mango chutney
6 ripe purple figs, sliced in half lengthwise
12oz/350g whole milk goat cheese, sliced
Salt and freshly ground black pepper

1 Preheat the broiler (grill). Spread both halves of the bread with mango chutney. Arrange slices of goat cheese and halves of fig alternately down the length of each half of bread. Season with salt and plenty of black pepper.

2 Broil the bruschetta until the cheese has melted a little and begun to brown around the edges, about 3–4 minutes. To serve, slice each piece of topped ciabatta widthwise in three, and place a piece on each serving plate. Serve immediately.

Cook's Tips

• Choose a round goat cheese that is firm enough to slice. Fresh mozzarella could be used instead, but will lack the delicious sharpness that makes the goat cheese such a fine foil for the figs.
• To make the cheese easier to slice, chill it briefly in the freezer.

Spiced Baby Eggplant

For a tempting first course, offer this with a simple salad of cucumber, chopped fresh green chiles, and chopped arugula (rocket).

SERVES 4

8oz/225g baby eggplant (aubergines)
2 tbsp garam masala
3 tbsp sunflower oil
2 tbsp/25g sweet butter
2 green cardamom pods
3 garlic cloves, chopped
2 tbsp chopped fresh ginger
1 tbsp cumin seeds
1 small onion, finely chopped
2 tbsp chopped fresh mint
Salt and freshly ground black pepper
1 lemon, cut into wedges, to serve

1 Hold the eggplant by the stalk ends and slice each lengthwise into 4 slices, leaving the slices attached at the stalk. Place the eggplant on a large plate and rub garam masala generously between the slices, taking care not to break the vegetables. Reserve the leftover garam masala.

2 Heat the oil and butter together in a skillet (frying pan). Split the cardamom pods and scrape the seeds into the pan. Add the garlic, ginger, cumin seeds, onion, and salt and pepper, and cook 5 minutes, stirring frequently, until the onion has softened but not browned.

3 Add the eggplant to the pan and sprinkle in the reserved garam masala. Cook 3 minutes, then turn the eggplant, and cook another 3 minutes. Pour enough hot water into the pan to just cover the base, stir it into the onion mixture between the eggplants.

4 When the water boils—almost immediately if it is hot enough—reduce the heat and cover the pan. Cook the eggplant another 5 minutes. Uncover the pan, turn the eggplant, and increase the heat. Simmer rapidly until all the water has evaporated, 3–4 minutes.

5 Transfer the eggplant to warm plates, flattening them slightly to splay the slices, and sprinkle with mint. Garnish with lemon wedges and serve immediately.

Goat Cheese & Zucchini Mousse

These pretty individual mousses are easy to make and absolutely delicious. Serve as an appetizer.

SERVES 4

11oz/300g fresh goat cheese
3oz/75g chèvre or sharp goat cheese
3 tbsp sour cream
2 extra large eggs
Small bunch fresh tarragon
2 zucchini (courgettes)
1 tbsp/15g butter
Salt and freshly ground black pepper

1 Preheat the oven to 375°F/190°C, Gas 5. Place both goat cheeses, the sour cream, eggs, and tarragon in a food processor. Season and blend until smooth.

2 Trim the zucchini and cut into thin strips lengthwise with a vegetable peeler. Grease four 6oz/175g dariole molds and line each one with strips of zucchini. Trim the ends if they protrude over the tops of the molds.

3 Spoon the cheese mixture into the molds and place them on a baking sheet.

4 Bake until firm, 20 minutes. Let rest for a couple of minutes, then unmold onto serving plates.

Roast Peppers

These tasty bell peppers make a wonderful first course. Serve with good bread to mop up the juices.

SERVES 4

2 large green bell peppers, seeded and
    quartered lengthwise
2 large red bell peppers, seeded and
    quartered lengthwise
Dressing
1 tbsp fennel seeds
2 bay leaves
6 tbsp extra-virgin olive oil
2 garlic cloves, finely chopped
1 tsp sugar
¼ cup/60ml sherry vinegar
Peel of 1 lemon, pared off in shreds
    using a zester
Salt and freshly ground black pepper
Handful fresh basil sprigs, shredded,
    to garnish
Lemon wedges, to serve

1 Preheat the broiler (grill). Place the quarters of green and red bell pepper skin-side up on the rack and broil until blackened and slightly softened, 5–7 minutes. Wrap in foil and let cool.

2 To make the dressing, roast the fennel seeds and bay leaves together in a small dry saucepan. Shake the pan frequently and remove from the heat as soon as the seeds begin to give off their aroma—do not overcook them or they will taste bitter. Add the olive oil and garlic to the hot pan, then set aside to cool.

3 Whisk the sugar, vinegar, and plenty of seasoning together in a bowl. Gradually whisk in the flavored oil. Stir in the lemon peel. Remove the bell peppers from the foil and peel carefully. Add them to the dressing, turning each piece to coat. Cover, and let marinate, 24 hours.

4 To serve, divide the green and red bell peppers evenly among four plates. Spoon the flavored oil, seeds, and lemon over them, but discard the bay leaves. Sprinkle with basil and add lemon wedges to serve.

Tomato & Basil Tartlets

These delightful little tartlets are incredibly easy to make, and would be a huge success at any dinner party.

MAKES 8 TARTLETS

12oz/350g ready-made puff pastry
Butter, for greasing
Filling
24–28 ripe cherry or baby plum
 tomatoes, halved
1 tsp finely chopped fresh rosemary
 or thyme
6 tbsp extra-virgin olive oil
Handful fresh basil leaves, plus extra
 to garnish
Salt and freshly ground black pepper

1 Preheat the oven to 400°F/200°C, Gas 6. Roll out half the pastry to an 8 x 17in/20 x 42cm rectangle and using a plain 4in/10cm cookie cutter, cut out eight rounds. Place onto a lightly greased baking sheet.

2 Divide the tomatoes among the rounds, leaving a ½in/1cm border. Sprinkle with the rosemary or thyme and drizzle with 2 tbsp of the olive oil. Season well and bake until the pastry is risen and golden, 12–15 minutes.

3 Meanwhile, put the remaining oil and basil in a blender or small food processor and blend until smooth. When the tartlets are cooked, drizzle with the basil mixture and garnish with basil leaves. Serve warm.

The Main Event

Truly mouthwatering meals

Quattro Formaggi Pizza
with walnuts

**The walnuts lend a tasty bite and texture
to an old favorite.**

MAKES TWO 9IN/23CM PIZZAS

2 garlic cloves, crushed
4 tbsp olive oil
2 large tomatoes, thinly sliced
2 tsp chopped fresh oregano
2 tbsp walnuts, chopped
5oz/150g mozzarella cheese, drained and
   torn into small pieces
2oz/50g Dolcelatte cheese, crumbled
4 tbsp freshly grated Parmesan cheese
5oz/150g Fontina cheese, sliced
Pizza dough
1½ cups/175g white bread flour
½ tsp salt
½ tsp rapid-rise dried yeast
½ cup/125ml lukewarm water
1 tbsp olive oil
Salt and freshly ground black pepper

1 To make the pizza dough, mix together
the flour, salt, and yeast. Stir in the water
and olive oil and mix to a soft dough,
starting off with a wooden spoon, then
bringing the dough together with your
hands. Turn the dough onto a lightly
floured surface. The texture will be very
rough and slightly sticky. Knead the dough
(folding it over itself and giving the dough
a quarter turn) until very smooth and
elastic, about 8–10 minutes.

2 Lightly grease a large bowl. Form the
dough into a neat ball and place it
carefully into the bowl. Rub a little oil over
the surface of the dough, or use an oil
mister and spray lightly. Cover with plastic
wrap and let rise at room temperature
until doubled in bulk, about 1 hour.

3 Remove the plastic wrap and tip the
dough onto a lightly floured surface. This
will deflate the dough. Knead another 2–3
minutes until smooth again.

4 Meanwhile, combine the garlic and
olive oil and set aside. Preheat the oven to
475°F/240°C, Gas 9 or its highest setting,
whichever is hotter. Put a pizza stone or
baking sheet on the highest shelf.

5 Divide the dough into two pieces and roll out each one to form a 9in/23cm round. Brush the pizza bases with the garlic and oil mixture. Top with the tomatoes, oregano, walnuts, and then the cheeses. Season well and drizzle with any remaining garlic oil.

6 Transfer the two pizzas to preheated pizza stones or baking sheets and bake one at a time in the top of the oven until the edges are golden brown, and the cheese topping has melted and is bubbling, 10–12 minutes. Let cool a few minutes before serving.

Pepper Tarte Tatin

This alternative version of the classic French tart looks and tastes wonderful.

SERVES 4

¾ cup/175g butter
1 cup/120g all-purpose (plain) flour
Generous cup/130g grated
  Cheddar cheese
2 tbsp water
Topping
2 tbsp olive oil, plus extra for greasing
2 garlic cloves, crushed
3 tomatoes, peeled, seeded, and diced
2 green (spring) onions, chopped
3¼ cups/225g chopped mushrooms
Grated peel of 1 lemon
3 red bell peppers, seeded and cut
  lengthwise into fine strips
Salt and freshly ground black pepper

1 Preheat the oven to 400°F/200°C, Gas 6. For the topping, heat the olive oil in a saucepan. Add the garlic, tomatoes, green onions, mushrooms, lemon peel, and season. Cook, stirring frequently, until the onions are tender and all the liquid produced by the mushrooms has evaporated, about 10 minutes. Let cool.

2 Grease an 8 x 2in/20 x 5cm round ovenproof dish with olive oil. Carefully arrange the strips of bell pepper in the dish, radiating from the center outward and packing them close together.

3 Carefully spoon the mushroom mixture on top of the bell peppers, piling it evenly. Use a knife to press the mixture down, leaving a gap all around the edge.

4 Rub the butter into the flour, then stir in the cheese and mix in the water to make a soft dough. Alternatively, process the flour, butter, and cheese together in a food processor, then mix in the water. Roll out the dough on a lightly floured surface to fit the top of the dish, allowing just a little extra. Lay it over the mushroom mixture, gently lifting the edge of the dough and tucking it inside the rim of the dish. Press the dough down neatly around the edge so that it is inside the dish.

5 Cut a slit in the middle of the dough for steam to escape, then bake until well browned, 35–40 minutes. Run a knife around the edge of the dish to loosen the pastry, then cover the dish with a platter, and invert. Gently lift the dish off the tart.

Onion Quiche

This simple quiche has a good clean flavor. Gorgeous when served with crisp salad greens to contrast with its luxurious creamy texture.

SERVES 6

½ cup/120g butter
1½ cups/175g all-purpose (plain) flour
2 tbsp cold water
Filling
2 tbsp/25g butter
1lb/450g onions, thinly sliced
3 eggs, beaten
1¼ cups/300ml light (single) cream
3 tbsp dry sherry
Pinch of ground mace
Salt and freshly ground black pepper

1 To make the dough, rub the butter into the flour until the mixture resembles fine bread crumbs. Stir in the cold water to bind the ingredients, then knead lightly. Wrap in plastic wrap and chill 30 minutes. Roll out the dough on a lightly floured surface and use to line a 10in/25cm loose-based tart pan (flan tin) or quiche dish. Prick the base all over and place in the refrigerator, another 30 minutes.

2 Preheat the oven to 400°F/200°C, Gas 6. Line the pie shell with waxed paper (baking parchment) and weigh down with baking beans or dried beans. Bake 10 minutes, then remove the beans and paper. Reduce the oven to 350°F/180°C, Gas 4.

3 Meanwhile, make the filling. Melt the butter in a heavy-based saucepan and add the onions. Stir well, then cook until softened but not browned, 10 minutes. Remove from the heat and cool slightly.

4 Beat the eggs with the cream, sherry, mace, and plenty of seasoning. Use a slotted spoon to transfer the cooked onions to the pie shell, distributing them evenly over the base, and pour any cooking juices into the egg mixture. Stir well, then pour the mixture over the onions. Bake the quiche until the filling is set and golden brown, about 45 minutes.

5 Let cool 15 minutes before serving. The quiche can be enjoyed warm or cold.

Spinach Roulade

This soft, puffy roulade is a delicious variation on the traditional soufflé. Serve sliced with mixed salad greens.

SERVES 6

6oz/175g fresh spinach
3 tbsp/45g butter, plus extra for greasing
3 tbsp/40g all-purpose (plain) flour, plus extra for dusting
1¾ cups/450ml milk
3 eggs, separated
¼ tsp grated nutmeg
4 tbsp freshly grated Parmesan cheese
7oz/200g garlic and herb cream cheese
⅓ cup/75g ricotta cheese
2 tbsp sour cream
2 tbsp chopped fresh chives
Salt and freshly ground black pepper

1 Preheat the oven to 400°F/200°C, Gas 6. Wash the spinach and cook in a covered saucepan until just wilted, 2–3 minutes. Cool slightly, squeeze out all the moisture, and finely chop. Grease and line a 9 x 13in/23 x 33cm jelly roll pan (Swiss roll tin) with waxed paper (baking parchment). Grease the paper and dust lightly with flour.

2 Melt the butter in a saucepan and stir in the flour. Cook 1 minute, then remove from the heat. Gradually whisk in the milk, then return to the heat, and continue whisking gently until the mixture boils and thickens. Boil 1 minute, then remove from the heat once more.

3 Whisk in the egg yolks one at a time until the mixture is smooth. Beat in the spinach, seasoning, and nutmeg.

4 Whisk the egg whites until they form stiff peaks and fold into the mixture. Pour the mixture into the pan (tin) and spread out evenly. Bake until lightly set, 12–14 minutes.

5 Sprinkle the Parmesan over a sheet of waxed paper and turn the roulade out onto it. Remove the lining paper and let cool slightly. Beat the garlic and herb cheese, ricotta, sour cream, and chives together. Spread the mixture over the roulade, then use the paper to roll it up from one long side.

Roast Vegetable Lasagna

This traditional multilayered Italian pasta dish is baked in the oven until bubbly and golden brown.

SERVES 4

1 large red bell pepper, seeded and cut into chunks
2 small zucchini (courgettes), cut into chunks
2 red onions, each cut into 8 wedges
6 garlic cloves, peeled
1 eggplant (aubergine), cut into chunks
2 tbsp olive oil
2 large fresh thyme sprigs
2 fresh bay leaves
2 x 11oz/300g jars fresh tomato sauce
11oz/300g jar artichokes in oil, drained and halved, if large
1 cup/50g sun-dried tomatoes
2¼ cups/500g ricotta cheese
4 tbsp freshly grated Parmesan cheese
2 eggs, beaten
11oz/300g lasagna sheets
Salt and freshly ground black pepper

1 Preheat the oven to 400°F/200°C, Gas 6. In a bowl, toss the bell pepper, zucchini, onions, whole garlic cloves, and eggplant in the olive oil. Tip everything into a large, shallow roasting pan. Tuck the thyme sprigs and bay leaves in among the vegetables. Cook near the top of the oven, turning once or twice, until tender and golden at the edges, 40 minutes. Reduce the oven to 375°F/190°C, Gas 5.

2 Remove the herbs. Mix the vegetables with the tomato sauce, artichokes, and sun-dried tomatoes.

3 Reserve about 3 tbsp of the Parmesan. In a large bowl, beat the ricotta until soft, then mix in the eggs, remaining Parmesan, and plenty of seasoning.

4 Spread a large spoonful of the vegetable mixture over the base of an ovenproof dish measuring 8 x 10 x 2½in (20 x 25 x 6cm.) Top with a layer of pasta, snapping the lasagna sheets to fit. Add half the remaining vegetables and top with half the remaining pasta. Add the last of the vegetable mixture and a final layer of pasta and top with the ricotta mixture. Sprinkle with the reserved Parmesan.

5 Bake in the center of the oven until bubbling and golden, 40–45 minutes.

Wide Noodles with roasted wild mushrooms, garlic, & parsley

Although a huge range of commercially prepared dried pasta is readily available, it is often inferior to good quality fresh pasta. Pasta should be cooked until "al dente"—meaning "to the tooth," or until still firm to the bite but without a hard, uncooked center.

SERVES 4

1lb/450g mixed wild mushrooms, wiped and sliced, if large
4 tbsp olive oil
2 garlic cloves, sliced
½ cup/125ml vegetable stock
½ cup/125ml heavy (double) cream
2 tbsp chopped fresh parsley
3 tbsp freshly grated Parmesan cheese, plus extra to serve
12oz/350g chili-flavored or plain fresh noodle pasta, such as pappardelle or tagliatelle
Salt and freshly ground black pepper

1 Preheat the oven to 400°F/200°C, Gas 6. Put the mushrooms in a shallow roasting pan and drizzle with 2 tbsp of the oil. Add the garlic and mix together. Place in the top of the oven and roast until the mushrooms are tender, but still firm.

2 Remove the mushrooms from the oven. Transfer to a large bowl. Place the roasting pan over a low heat on the stove (hob) and add the vegetable stock, stirring well to scrape up any sediment from the mushrooms. Bring to a boil and cook until reduced by half. Stir in the cream, parsley, and Parmesan. Add the mushrooms and simmer briefly.

3 Bring a large pan of salted water to a boil. Add the pasta and cook following the packet instructions until al dente. Drain well. Top the pasta with the mushroom sauce and extra grated Parmesan and season to taste.

Parsley & Leek Frittata

This Italian version of an omelet is very easy to make. It makes a wonderful, light lunch with salad greens or rolled up and served as part of a picnic.

SERVES 4

2 tbsp/25g butter
3 leeks, thinly sliced at a slant
2 small bunches fresh parsley, stalks
  removed and finely chopped
4 extra large eggs, beaten
Salt and freshly ground black pepper

1 Melt the butter in a medium-size skillet (frying pan) and add the leeks. Cook until soft, 8–10 minutes. Add the parsley, and stir to combine.

2 Season the eggs. Pour the eggs into the skillet and cook gently, about 10 minutes. The base of the frittata should be set, but the top will still be wobbly.

3 Place the skillet under a preheated broiler (grill) and broil until the top is set and golden, 3–4 minutes.

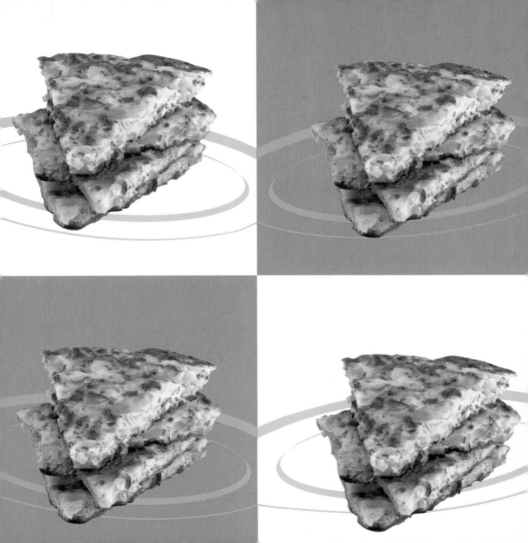

Risotto Primavera

To make the perfect risotto, you don't
have to stand over it stirring like crazy—
stirring every now and then when you
add the stock still gives great results.

SERVES 6

2 tbsp/25g butter
1 tbsp olive oil
1 onion, finely chopped
1 stalk celery, finely chopped
2 carrots, finely chopped
1¾ cups/400g risotto rice
4 cups/1 liter vegetable stock
¾ cup/75g shelled fresh peas
2 zucchini (courgettes), finely chopped
Small bunch fresh mint, finely chopped
Small bunch fresh parsley, finely chopped
Salt and freshly ground black pepper
Shavings of fresh Parmesan cheese,
   to serve

1 Melt the butter with the oil in a large
heavy-based saucepan and add the
vegetables. Cover and cook, 15 minutes.

2 Add the rice to the pan and stir well to
coat. Add about ½ cup/125ml stock and stir.
Cook until the liquid has been absorbed.

3 Add the same amount of stock and the
peas, stir a few times, and again let the
rice cook and absorb the liquid. Continue
in this way leaving ½ cup/125ml stock in
reserve, about 25 minutes.

4 Stir the zucchini into the risotto with
the remaining stock. Stir well and season.

5 When the zucchini are tender, stir the
herbs into the risotto. This dish does not
like to hang around, so serve immediately
topped with shavings of Parmesan.

Cheese Soufflé

After mixing, the soufflé mixture can be kept in a refrigerator for an hour or two, but the soufflé should be served immediately after baking as the dramatic rise won't last for ever. This cheese soufflé has a crisp Parmesan crust and a delicious soft center.

SERVES 4

¼ cup/60g butter, plus extra for greasing
½ cup/55g all-purpose (plain) flour
1 cup/250ml milk
Pinch of freshly grated nutmeg
¼ tsp hot mustard powder
2 cups/225g grated Cheddar cheese
5 eggs, separated
1 tbsp freshly grated Parmesan cheese
Salt and freshly ground black pepper

1 Preheat the oven to 350°F/180°C, Gas 4. Grease a 6 cup/1.5 liter soufflé dish with butter. Melt the remaining butter in a large heavy-based saucepan, stir in the flour, and cook 1 minute. Remove from the heat, whisk in the milk, then bring to a boil, whisking until the sauce has thickened. Remove from the heat and add the nutmeg, mustard powder, and seasoning. Stir in the Cheddar and let cool a few minutes.

2 Whisk the egg yolks into the sauce, one at a time until well incorporated and the sauce is smooth and glossy.

3 Whisk the egg whites until they form stiff peaks. Stir 1 tbsp of the egg whites into the sauce to slacken it slightly, then gently fold in the rest.

4 Pour the mixture into the soufflé dish and run your finger around the top inside edge. Sprinkle with Parmesan and bake until golden and risen, 30–40 minutes.

Mushroom & Garlic Soufflé

Use mushrooms with a good strong flavor and a low water content such as chestnut or portabello mushrooms, as they will give the best result. This recipe is delightful when served with mixed salad greens.

SERVES 4

1½ tbsp/20g butter, plus extra for greasing
3 tbsp/20g all-purpose (plain) flour
1 cup/250ml milk
Pinch of grated nutmeg
2oz/50g mild goat cheese
4 eggs, separated

Flavoring

1 tbsp/15g butter
11oz/300g chestnut or portabello
  mushrooms, halved and thinly sliced
2 garlic cloves, crushed
2 tbsp chopped fresh parsley
1 tsp fresh thyme leaves
Salt and freshly ground black pepper

1 Preheat the oven to 375°F/190°C, Gas 5. Grease a 6 cup/1.5 liter soufflé dish with butter. Melt the remaining butter in a large saucepan, add the flour, and cook, 1 minute. Remove from the heat, whisk in the milk, then bring to a boil, whisking until the sauce has thickened. Remove from the heat and add the nutmeg and seasoning. Stir in the goat cheese and let cool a few minutes.

2 For the flavoring, melt the butter in a large skillet (frying pan) add the mushrooms and cook over medium heat until softened and all the liquid has evaporated. Stir in the garlic, cook 1 minute, then let cool.

3 Whisk the egg yolks into the sauce, one at a time until well incorporated and the sauce is smooth and glossy. Stir in the mushrooms and herbs.

4 Whisk the egg whites until they form stiff peaks. Stir 1 tbsp of the egg whites into the sauce to slacken it slightly, then gently fold in the rest.

5 Pour the mixture into the soufflé dish. Run your finger around the inside edge, and bake, 30–40 minutes.

Pappardelle with zucchini, sun-dried tomatoes, & pine nuts

Pappardelle is a long, flat, wide pasta typical of Tuscany, but also prepared in Umbria and other regions of Italy. The word "pappardelle" comes from the Tuscan word "pappare," literally meaning "to gobble up!"

SERVES 4

3 tbsp extra-virgin olive oil
1 tbsp pine nuts
2 garlic cloves, sliced
2 zucchini (courgettes), thinly sliced
Large pinch of chili flakes
2 tsp grated lemon peel
4 sun-dried tomatoes, chopped
12oz/350g fresh pappardelle pasta
Handful fresh basil leaves, coarsely torn
Salt and freshly ground black pepper
Freshly grated Parmesan cheese, to serve

1 Heat 1 tbsp of the oil in a large skillet (frying pan). Add the pine nuts and garlic, and cook gently until golden. Remove from the skillet with a slotted spoon and drain on paper towels. Set aside.

2 Add an additional 1 tbsp of the oil and the zucchini. Increase the heat slightly and cook, stirring occasionally, until golden, about 5 minutes. Return the pine nuts and garlic to the pan with the chili flakes, lemon peel, and sun-dried tomatoes. Cook until heated through, about 1 minute.

3 Meanwhile, bring a large saucepan of salted water to a rolling boil. Add the pasta and cook following the packet instructions until al dente. Drain, reserving a little of the water.

4 Add the pasta to the skillet with the zucchini along with the basil. Season well and mix together, adding a little of the reserved water if it seems a little dry. Divide among serving plates and top with a sprinkling of freshly grated Parmesan. Serve immediately.

Ratatouille Provencal

Classic ratatouille is a dish of roasted vegetables lightly covered in a rich sauce. Serve it hot or cold. To complete the meal, top with slices of smoked mozzarella and place under the broiler (grill) until golden.

SERVES 4

2 bulbs fennel, quartered lengthwise
3 red onions, quartered
6 garlic cloves, whole and unpeeled
6 tbsp olive oil
3 zucchini (courgettes), cut into
½in/1cm slices
2 red bell peppers, seeded and cut
into chunks
1 eggplant (aubergine), cut into 2in/
5cm chunks
Tomato sauce
14oz/400g can chopped tomatoes
½ cup/125ml white wine
2 tbsp tomato paste
6 fresh thyme sprigs
1 tsp sugar
Salt and freshly ground black pepper

1 Preheat the oven to 400°F/200°C, Gas 6. You will need two large roasting pans for this. Don't try to cram all the vegetables into one or they'll end up soggy and stewed instead of roasted.

2 Blanch the fennel in boiling water, 5 minutes. Drain, and place in a roasting pan with the onions, three unpeeled garlic cloves, and half the oil. Season well and roast in the top of the oven, 50 minutes.

3 Meanwhile, put the zucchini, bell peppers, and eggplant into the second roasting pan. Pour the remaining oil over the vegetables, add the remaining unpeeled garlic cloves, and roast on the second shelf of the oven, 40 minutes.

4 To make the tomato sauce, empty the tomatoes into a saucepan and stir in the remaining ingredients. Simmer until reduced and thickened, 20 minutes. Remove the thyme sprigs and stir the roasted vegetables into the tomato sauce. Serve immediately.

Chow Mein with snow peas

Snow peas bring crunch and color to tender Chinese egg noodles. This chow mein is delicious for a simple, healthy midweek supper.

SERVES 4

6 large dried shiitake mushrooms
12oz/350g dried Chinese egg noodles
2 tsp cornstarch (cornflour)
6 tbsp dry sherry
2 tbsp light soy sauce
2 tsp sesame oil
2 tbsp safflower oil
2 tbsp chopped fresh ginger
2 garlic cloves, crushed
8oz/225g snow peas, sliced
8 green onions, finely chopped
Freshly ground black pepper
3 tbsp chopped fresh cilantro (coriander),
  to garnish

1 Place the mushrooms in a small bowl and pour in just enough boiling water to cover them. Let soak 10 minutes, pressing the mushrooms into the water frequently so that they rehydrate. Drain and slice the mushrooms, reserving the soaking water and discarding any tough stems.

2 Place the dried egg noodles in a large bowl, breaking the sheets in half so that they fit easily, cover with plenty of boiling water. Cover and let soak 10 minutes, until tender. Blend the cornstarch to a smooth paste with the sherry, soy sauce, and sesame oil. Prepare a colander or strainer for draining the noodles before beginning to stir-fry the vegetables.

3 Heat the safflower oil in a wok or large skillet (frying pan). Add the ginger and stir-fry 30 seconds, then add the garlic, and stir-fry another 30 seconds. Add the mushrooms and cook briefly, then add the snow peas and green onions. Stir-fry 1 minute. Pour in the cornstarch mixture and bring to a boil, stirring until thickened.

4 Drain the noodles and add them to the vegetables. Toss all the ingredients together so that they are thoroughly combined. Taste for seasoning and add more soy sauce to taste if necessary, then sprinkle the chopped cilantro over the chow mein and serve immediately.

Baked Spinach Gnocchi

Here, spinach, garlic, a little olive oil, and some Parmesan cheese bring fabulous flavor to the simplest gnocchi, which is light and crisp when cooked.

SERVES 4

3 tbsp extra-virgin olive oil, plus
    extra for greasing
2 green (spring) onions, chopped
1 garlic clove, crushed
8oz/225g fresh spinach
2 cups/500ml milk
⅔ cup/120g semolina
Freshly grated nutmeg
1 egg, beaten
¾ cup/60g freshly grated Parmesan cheese
Salt and freshly ground black pepper

1 Heat the olive oil, green onions, and garlic together in a large saucepan. When the onions begin to sizzle, add the spinach and stir well. Cover and cook until the spinach wilts, 30 seconds. Stir for a few seconds, then remove from the heat.

2 Cool the spinach slightly, then transfer the mixture to a food processor, scraping all the liquid, green onions, and garlic from the pan, and chop finely. If you do not have a food processor, use a blender to puree the mixture, or drain bundles of the mixture, reserving all the liquid, and chop them by hand, then return them to the reserved juices.

3 Pour the milk into the pan used to cook the spinach (there is no need to wash it) and heat until boiling. Gradually sprinkle in the semolina, stirring all the time. Cook until the mixture boils, first stirring, then beating as it thickens. After about 1 minute, the semolina should be very thick and come away from the sides of the pan. Remove from the heat and stir in the spinach mixture. Add salt, pepper, and nutmeg to taste. Let cool slightly, then beat in the egg.

4 Grease a shallow dish with a little olive oil, or line a baking sheet with plastic wrap. Turn the semolina mixture out onto it, spreading the mixture out to a rectangle measuring about 7 x 10in/18 x 25cm. Neaten the edges by patting them with a knife, then cover with plastic wrap, and set aside to cool. Chill 2–4 hours or overnight.

5 Preheat the oven to 400°F/200°C, Gas 6 and grease a 10in/25cm round ovenproof dish with a little olive oil. (A tart pan or quiche dish is fine for this.) Use a large kitchen knife to cut the semolina gnocchi into three strips slightly more than 2in/5cm wide. Wet the knife under cold running water to prevent the mixture from sticking to it, then wipe with a paper towel; wet it again between cuts. Cut the mixture at 2in/5cm intervals in the opposite direction, to yield 15 squares.

6 Carefully dip each square in grated Parmesan to coat both sides, and place in the dish. Overlap the squares around the edge of the dish, then place a few in the middle to fill it neatly. Sprinkle with any remaining Parmesan and bake until crisp and golden on top, about 30 minutes. Serve immediately.

Goat Cheese & Arugula Omelet

This savory version of a soufflé omelet makes a really simple, light but delicious supper. With a topping of goat cheese, tomatoes, arugula (rocket), and olives, it has an authentic Mediterranean flavor.

SERVES 1–2

3 eggs
¼ tsp fresh thyme leaves
2 tbsp freshly grated Parmesan cheese
1 tbsp/15g butter
Filling
6 cherry tomatoes, sliced
6 pitted black olives, sliced
3oz/75g mild soft goat cheese
Handful of arugula or baby spinach
   leaves, washed
1 tsp vinaigrette dressing
Salt and freshly ground black pepper

1 Break 2 eggs into a bowl. Separate the remaining egg, and add the yolk to the 2 eggs, reserving the egg white. Using a hand-held electric mixer, whisk the eggs until thick and foamy. Clean the beaters and whisk the egg white in a separate bowl until it forms stiff peaks.

2 Fold the egg white into the whisked eggs with the thyme leaves, Parmesan, and some seasoning. Melt the butter in a small skillet (frying pan) and pour in the egg mixture. Cook over medium heat until golden underneath, 1–2 minutes.

3 Put the pan under a hot broiler (grill) and broil until golden, 1 minute. Top one half with the tomatoes and olives, then dot over spoonfuls of the goat cheese. Toss the arugula in the dressing and add to the omelet. Flip over the uncovered half of the omelet and slide onto a plate to serve.

Kohlrabi & Feta Strudel

Here, a simple vegetable mixture is transformed into an impressive lunch or supper dish when rolled in a crisp phyllo (filo) pastry coat.

SERVES 4-6

2 tbsp olive oil, plus extra for greasing
2 tbsp/25g butter, melted
8 sheets phyllo (filo) pastry, about 14 x 8in/
   35 x 20cm each
4 tbsp fine dry white bread crumbs

Filling

1lb/450g kohlrabi, peeled and cut into
   ½in/1cm cubes
6 green (spring) onions, chopped
3 tbsp chopped fresh parsley
8oz/225g feta cheese, finely crumbled
Pinch of freshly grated nutmeg
Freshly ground black pepper

1 To make the filling, cook the kohlrabi in boiling salted water for 5 minutes, then drain, and transfer to a bowl. Let cool slightly until warm before mixing in the green onions, parsley, and feta cheese. Add a little nutmeg and pepper. The feta is salty so the mixture should not need additional salt.

2 Preheat the oven to 350°F/180°C, Gas 4. Grease a large baking sheet with a little oil.

3 Mix together the butter and oil. Lay a sheet of phyllo pastry on a clean, dry work surface and brush lightly with a little of the butter and oil mixture. Lay a second sheet with the long side overlapping the long side of the first piece by about a third. (This will give an area of pastry measuring about 14 x 13½in/35 x 34cm.) Brush the second sheet with butter and oil. Lay the remaining sheets on top, overlapping them as before and brushing sparingly with butter and oil.

4 Sprinkle the bread crumbs over the pastry and top with the kohlrabi and feta mixture, spooning it on evenly, leaving a 2in/5cm border. Fold the edge of the phyllo over the filling, then brush the edge with a little butter and oil. Roll up the phyllo and filling like a jelly roll (Swiss roll). Transfer to the baking sheet, bending the roll if necessary to make it fit. Brush with butter and oil, and bake until crisp and golden, 40–45 minutes. Let stand 5 minutes before cutting into thick slices.

Mushroom Tart
with walnut pastry

This exquisite tart can be served either hot or chilled, and makes an invaluable addition to a midsummer picnic.

SERVES 6

½ cup/50g walnuts
1½ cups/175g all-purpose (plain) flour
Pinch of salt
Generous ⅓ cup/85g butter, diced
2–3 tbsp cold water
Filling
2 tbsp/25g butter
1 tbsp vegetable oil
1 small onion, finely chopped
12oz/350g mixed fresh wild or
    cultivated mushrooms
2 garlic cloves, finely chopped
Pinch of freshly grated nutmeg
2 egg yolks
1 cup/250ml heavy (double) cream
1 tbsp chopped fresh parsley
Freshly ground black pepper

1 Grind the walnuts in a food processor or spice grinder until fine, but not pasty— if you overgrind them, they will become very oily and sticky which will make the pastry very difficult to handle.

2 Sift the flour into a mixing bowl with the salt. Add the butter and, using your fingertips, rub it into the flour until the mixture resembles coarse bread crumbs. Mix the ground nuts into the mixture. Add 2 tbsp of the water and using your hands, bring the dough together, adding a little more water, if necessary. Form the dough into a ball, wrap in plastic wrap and chill, 30 minutes.

3 Preheat the oven to 400°F/200°C, Gas 6. Roll out the dough on a lightly floured work surface and use it to line a 9in/23cm loose-based pastry ring or tart pan (flan tin). Prick the base with a fork, line the pastry with waxed paper (baking parchment) and fill with baking beans. Bake 12 minutes. Remove the lining and baking beans and cook an additional 10 minutes until golden. Remove from the oven and set aside to cool. Reduce the oven temperature to 350°F/180°C, Gas 4.

4 Heat the butter and oil in a large skillet (frying pan). Add the onion and cook until softened, about 5 minutes. Increase the heat and add the mushrooms. Cook until softened, another 4–5 minutes. Add the garlic, nutmeg, and seasoning. Stir briefly and remove from the heat.

5 Spoon the mushroom mixture evenly over the pie shell. Whisk the egg yolks, cream, parsley, and seasoning together. Pour evenly over the mushrooms. Bake until just set, 30–35 minutes. Let cool 15 minutes before serving. Serve warm or at room temperature.

On The Side

Alluring additions and side plates

Maple-baked Acorn Squash

Winter squashes, such as acorn, butternut, and pumpkin, are available just at the right time for the New England maple syrup harvest. The syrup sweetly complements these popular winter vegetables.

SERVES 4

2 medium or small acorn squash
2 tbsp/25g butter
¼ cup/60ml pure natural maple syrup
¼ tsp salt
¼ tsp ground cinnamon
⅛ tsp allspice
¼ cup/30g chopped pecans or
  walnuts (optional)

1 Preheat the oven to 350°F/180°C, Gas 4.

2 Cut each squash in half lengthwise, then scoop out their seeds and fibers. Use a sharp knife to slice off a small piece of each base. Arrange the squash halves, cut-side down, in an ovenproof dish and cover with foil. Bake about 30 minutes, until the squash begins to soften.

3 Turn the squash cut-side up and divide the butter, maple syrup, salt, and spices equally among them. Sprinkle each one with nuts, if using. Bake, uncovered, until the squash are tender, about 20 minutes.

Spiced Zucchini

Zesty cardamom goes well with subtle-tasting zucchini and rich coconut in this simple spiced dish.

SERVES 4

2 tbsp/25g butter
1 onion, finely chopped
8 green cardamom pods
2 tsp cumin seeds
1 bay leaf
1½lb/675g zucchini, peeled, halved, and seeded, cut into 1in/2.5cm chunks
1 cup/250ml coconut milk
½ cup/125ml plain strained yogurt or crème fraîche
2 green (spring) onions, finely chopped
2 tbsp chopped fresh cilantro (coriander)
Salt and freshly ground black pepper

1 Melt the butter in a saucepan. Add the onion.

2 Add the cardamom, making a slit in each pod and crushing it slightly as you add it to the pan. Stir in the cumin seeds and bay leaf, then cover the pan, and cook gently for 15 minutes.

3 Stir in the zucchini with seasoning. Continue stirring until the zucchini is thoroughly combined with the onion and spices. Then pour in the coconut milk and heat until simmering. Simmer, uncovered, for 15 minutes or until the zucchini is tender. Stir the zucchini frequently so that the pieces cook evenly.

4 Stir in the yogurt or crème fraîche and immediately remove the pan from the heat. Add more seasoning, if necessary. Remove the bay leaf and serve immediately, sprinkled with the green onions and fresh cilantro.

Roasted Vegetables
with pine nuts & parmesan

Roasted vegetables take on a wonderful intensity of flavor. The pine nut and cheese crumb topping finishes off this dish perfectly.

SERVES 4

4 tbsp olive oil
8 small new potatoes, halved or quartered
    lengthwise, if large
4 small parsnips, halved or quartered
    lengthwise, if large
6 baby leeks, trimmed
4 asparagus spears, trimmed
¼ cup/20g freshly grated Parmesan cheese
2 tbsp pine nuts, toasted
¼ cup/15g fresh white bread crumbs
Salt and freshly ground black pepper

1 Preheat the oven to 400°F/200°C, Gas 6. Pour the oil into a roasting pan, add the potatoes and parsnips, and toss well to coat in the oil. Season and roast in the oven, 30 minutes.

2 Add the leeks and asparagus to the roasting pan. Toss all the vegetables together, return to the oven, and roast another 25 minutes.

3 Put the Parmesan in a food processor with the pine nuts and bread crumbs. Blend for a couple of seconds until the nuts are coarsely chopped.

4 Sprinkle the mixture over the roasted vegetables and return to the oven until crispy and golden, another 5 minutes.

Jerusalem Artichokes
with basil & olives

Pungent basil and rich black olives taste terrific when combined with simply cooked Jerusalem artichokes.

SERVES 4

1½lb/675g Jerusalem artichokes, scrubbed
Juice of ½ lemon
12 large fresh basil sprigs, finely shredded
2 tbsp chopped fresh chives
12 black olives, pitted and thinly sliced
¼ cup/60ml extra-virgin olive oil
Salt and freshly ground black pepper
4 lemon wedges, to serve

1 Cook the Jerusalem artichokes in boiling salted water until tender, about 10 minutes. Drain well, then cut the artichokes into fairly thick slices. Arrange the slices neatly in a warm serving dish and sprinkle with lemon juice.

2 Season the artichokes well with freshly ground black pepper. Sprinkle with the basil, chives, and black olives, then trickle the olive oil evenly over the top. Serve immediately, with the lemon wedges.

3 If you want to serve this dish as a cold salad, cover the dish and set aside until the artichokes have cooled, then chill in the refrigerator, 30 minutes. Turn the artichokes in the olive oil before serving.

Broccoli Pilaf

Fragrant basmati rice and crisp broccoli are carefully spiced in this simple pilaf, which makes an excellent addition to any number of Indian dishes.

SERVES 4

1 generous cup/240g basmati rice
1lb/450g small broccoli flowerets
2 tbsp sunflower oil
2 onions, thinly sliced
2 garlic cloves, crushed
2 stalks celery, thinly sliced
2 tbsp cumin seeds
8 green cardamom pods
1 bay leaf
1 cinnamon stick
1 tsp saffron threads
Salt and freshly ground black pepper

1 Place the basmati rice in a bowl. Pour in plenty of cold water, then swirl the grains gently, let them settle, and pour off the cloudy water. Repeat this process several times until the water runs clear. Cover with fresh cold water and set aside to soak for 30 minutes.

2 Boil the broccoli in a large saucepan of water for 2 minutes. Drain the broccoli, reserving the vegetable stock.

3 Heat the oil in a skillet (frying pan). Add the onions, garlic, celery, cumin seeds, cardamom pods, bay leaf, and cinnamon stick. Stir, then cook 10 minutes stirring occasionally, until the onions have softened and are beginning to brown.

4 Meanwhile, drain the rice and set it aside in the strainer. When the onions are cooked, add the rice to the pan and pour in the reserved stock. Add salt and pepper, then bring to a boil over high heat and stir once. Cover the pan and reduce the heat to the lowest setting. Cook 10 minutes.

5 While the rice is cooking, pound the saffron threads in a mortar with a pestle and stir in 2 tbsp boiling water. Sprinkle the saffron water over the rice, then add the broccoli, leaving it piled on top of the rice. Quickly re-cover the pan and cook for another 5 minutes. Remove from the heat and let stand, without removing the lid, 5 minutes. Fluff the rice with a fork and mix in the broccoli. Serve immediately.

Braised Fennel

**This simple side dish can also be topped
with bread crumbs and cheese, then
broiled (grilled) until crisp to make a
delicious first course or light lunch.**

SERVES 4

2 tbsp/25g butter
1 small onion, finely chopped
1 small carrot, finely chopped
4 fennel bulbs, halved lengthwise
2 cups/500ml medium dry white wine
Salt and freshly ground black pepper

1 Preheat the oven to 400°F/200°C,
Gas 6. Melt the butter in a flameproof
casserole dish. Add the onion and carrot.
Season and cook on the stovetop (hob),
stirring, 5 minutes.

2 Add the fennel to the casserole, flat-
side down, cook 2 minutes, then pour in
the wine. Heat until simmering, basting
the fennel with the wine. Cover and
transfer to the oven. Cook about
40 minutes, turning the fennel after
30 minutes, until the bulbs are completely
tender. Taste and adjust the seasoning
before serving.

Pumpkin Couscous

This simple pumpkin and garbanzo (chickpea) sauce is deliciously aromatic and absolutely perfect with the light, fluffy couscous.

SERVES 4

3 tbsp olive oil
2 garlic cloves, crushed
2 onions, finely chopped
1 green bell pepper, seeded and chopped
1 yellow bell pepper, seeded and chopped
1 tbsp dried sage
2lb/900g prepared pumpkin, cut into ½in/1cm cubes
2 x 14oz/400g cans chopped tomatoes
14oz/400g can garbanzos, drained
1⅓ cups/225g couscous
1 large mild green chile, such as Anaheim, seeded and chopped
1 hot chile, such as jalapeño or serrano, seeded and chopped
Grated peel of 1 lemon
3 tbsp chopped fresh parsley
A little extra-virgin olive oil (optional)
Salt and freshly ground black pepper

1 Heat the olive oil in a saucepan. Add the garlic, onions, and green and yellow bell peppers. Stir well, then cover the pan, and cook over medium heat until the vegetables have softened, 15 minutes.

2 Stir in the sage and pumpkin, then pour in the tomatoes with their juice. Mix in the garbanzos and season. Bring to a boil, reduce the heat, and cover. Simmer 25–30 minutes.

3 When the pumpkin has been cooking 5–10 minutes, place the couscous in a heatproof bowl. Sprinkle with a little salt. Pour in 1¾ cups/450ml boiling water, cover, and let stand 15 minutes. In a separate bowl, mix the mild and hot chiles with the lemon peel and parsley.

4 Taste the pumpkin and season if necessary. Add the chile, lemon, and parsley mixture and remove from the heat. Stir lightly. Fluff the couscous with a fork and drizzle with a little extra-virgin olive oil, if using, then season with freshly ground black pepper. Divide the couscous among four large warmed bowls. Ladle the pumpkin casserole over the couscous and serve immediately.

Parsnip & Blue Cheese Mash

Tangy blue cheese goes well with sweet parsnips, and this mash makes an unorthodox but delicious side dish.

SERVES 4

1½lb/675g young parsnips, trimmed and cut into chunks
2 tbsp/25g butter
1 onion, chopped
1 leek, chopped
2 tbsp finely chopped fresh ginger
3 tbsp chopped fresh parsley
8oz/225g blue cheese, such as Roquefort, Stilton, Gorgonzola, or Dolcelatte, crumbled
Salt and freshly ground black pepper

1 Cook the parsnips in salted boiling water until tender, about 15 minutes. Meanwhile, melt the butter in a saucepan and add the onion, leek, and ginger with plenty of salt and pepper. Stir well, cover, and cook 15 minutes, stirring occasionally, until the leek and onion have softened but not browned.

2 Drain and mash the parsnips until smooth. Stir in the leek and onion mixture with all the juices from the pan. Beat in the parsley, then lightly mix in the blue cheese. Taste for seasoning, then serve immediately.

Mash with olives, garlic, & dill

This fabulous mash makes a satisfying, full-flavored side dish. A fine accompaniment to a crisp fresh salad.

SERVES 4

2¼lb/1kg potatoes, peeled and cut into chunks
5 tbsp extra-virgin olive oil
1 garlic clove, chopped
4–6 tbsp light (single) cream or milk
½ cup/15g fresh dill, chopped
8 black olives, pitted and chopped
Salt and freshly ground black pepper

1 Place the potatoes in a saucepan and pour in enough boiling water to cover them. Add a little salt and return to the boil. Reduce the heat, cover the pan, and cook until the potatoes are tender, about 10 minutes. Drain well.

2 Return the potatoes to the pan and add the olive oil, together with plenty of freshly ground black pepper. Mash the potatoes until smooth. Beat in the garlic, cream or milk, dill, and olives. Taste for seasoning and serve immediately.

Patatas Bravas

These "fierce potatoes" are a regular feature on Spanish tapas menus. Serve them as part of a tapas meal or as an accompaniment to an omelet or fresh green salad.

SERVES 4

5 potatoes, peeled and cut into
  1in/2.5cm cubes
6 tbsp olive oil
1 red onion, chopped
3 garlic cloves, chopped
1 tbsp paprika
Pinch or more of chili flakes
14oz/400g can chopped tomatoes
1 tbsp chopped fresh oregano

1 Parboil the potatoes in salted boiling water, 5 minutes, then drain well.

2 Heat 4 tbsp oil in a large skillet (frying pan), add the potatoes, and fry slowly over a medium heat, 15 minutes. Transfer the potatoes to an ovenproof serving dish and keep warm in a moderate oven.

3 Heat the remaining oil in the skillet and cook the onion and garlic until golden, 10 minutes. Add the paprika and chili flakes and cook another 2 minutes. Drain most of the excess juice from the tomatoes, then add them to the fried onion mixture. Cook 5 minutes, then stir in the oregano, and pour the tomato sauce over the potatoes.

Spinach with paneer

This simple dish of spiced spinach with light cheese makes a terrific vegetarian side dish. Serve it with basmati rice, Indian-style lentils, and naan bread.

SERVES 4

2 tbsp/25g butter or ghee
8oz/225g paneer, in one piece
1 large onion, chopped
1 garlic clove, crushed
1 tbsp cumin seeds
1 tsp ground turmeric
2¼lb/1kg young spinach, coarsely shredded
Salt and freshly ground black pepper

1 Melt the butter or ghee in a heavy-based saucepan. Add the paneer and cook until it is golden brown underneath, then use a spatula to turn it, and cook the other side. Remove from the pan, drain carefully, and transfer to a plate.

2 Add the onion, garlic, and cumin seeds to the pan. Stir well, then cook over medium heat until the onion has thoroughly softened and is beginning to brown in places, about 15 minutes. Stir frequently and keep the heat fairly low.

3 Stir in the turmeric with plenty of salt and pepper. Add the spinach to the pan and cover tightly. Cook 2 minutes, until the spinach has wilted. Meanwhile, cut the paneer into small cubes.

4 Stir the spinach with the onion and cooking juices. Taste and adjust the seasoning. Top with the paneer and cook 2 minutes to heat the cheese slightly.

Stir-fried Brown Rice & Vegetables

Simple, healthy, and truly delicious!

SERVES 4

2 cups/450g short-grain brown rice
Pinch of salt
½ cup sesame seeds
Small handful dried arame seaweed
Sesame oil
2 onions, finely diced
2 tsp soy sauce
2 carrots, sliced into batons
¼in/5mm strips nori seaweed or finely
   chopped parsley, to garnish

1 Wash the rice under cold running water, to allow any debris or chaff to overflow. In a heavy-based saucepan combine the rice with 4 cups/1 liter cold water and the salt. Bring to a rapid boil without the lid, cover, and reduce the heat. Cook 30–35 minutes until tender.

2 Meanwhile, wash the sesame seeds in a strainer under running water, then empty into a heavy skillet (frying pan) and cook over medium heat, stirring, until they turn golden brown and a few of them begin to pop and crackle. Remove and let cool.

3 Soak the arame in a bowl of water, 5–6 minutes. Remove the arame from the water and squeeze out any excess liquid.

4 Cover the surface of a clean heavy skillet with sesame oil. Turn up the heat a little and sauté the onions with half the soy sauce until they are translucent. Add the carrots and continue to stir. Add the arame seaweed to the onions and carrots then stir-fry 2 minutes.

5 Slowly add the cooked brown rice to the pan and stir to prevent the mixture from sticking. If you feel the dish needs more liquid, add the water used for soaking the arame. Continue stirring until the rice is hot. Add the remaining soy sauce during the final minute, and mix in the sesame seeds.

6 Garnish with nori seaweed or finely chopped parsley and serve immediately.

Stir-fried Greens

The secret to serving perfect greens is speedy cooking. These are fresh and lively: serve with plain egg noodles to make a simple, healthy supper.

SERVES 4

2 tbsp sunflower oil
8 green (spring) onions, chopped
12oz/350g bok choy (pak choi), thinly sliced
4oz/115g Chinese cabbage, thinly sliced
4oz/115g baby spinach leaves
Handful of mizuna leaves, shredded
2 tbsp light soy sauce, or to taste
A few drops of sesame oil (optional)

1 Heat the sunflower oil in a wok or large saucepan. Add the green onions, bok choy, and Chinese cabbage. Stir-fry until the vegetables have wilted, 2–3 minutes. Add the spinach and cook for another minute, or until wilted. Stir in the mizuna and add the light soy sauce to taste.

2 Remove the greens from the heat and stir in a few drops of sesame oil, if desired. Serve immediately.

Coleslaw

Coleslaw is everybody's favorite, and if you've never made your own, you will be surprised at the creamy subtlety of flavors compared to supermarket brands which tend to be soggy and acidic.

SERVES 8–10

1 white cabbage
2 carrots
1 stalk celery, finely chopped
1 dessert apple, cored and finely chopped
⅓ cup/50g raisins
Small bunch fresh chives, chopped
Dressing
½ cup/125ml mayonnaise
1 cup/225ml plain yogurt
1 tsp white wine vinegar
Salt and freshly ground black pepper

1 Slice the cabbage and carrots on the fine julienne blade of a mandoline and mix together in a large bowl.

2 Add the celery and apple to the cabbage along with the raisins and stir well. Mix the chives into the coleslaw.

3 To make the dressing, mix the mayonnaise, yogurt, and vinegar together and season. Pour the dressing over the coleslaw and toss together. Chill until ready to serve.

Table of Equivalents

The following conversions and equivalents will provide useful guidelines for international readers to follow. There's just one golden rule to remember when you're preparing your ingredients: always stay with one system of measurement—that way you'll achieve the best results from these recipes.

Liquid Measures

½ tsp	=	2.5ml
1 tsp	=	5ml
2 tsp	=	10ml
1 tbsp	=	15ml
¼ cup	=	60ml
⅓ cup	=	75ml
½ cup	=	125ml
⅔ cup	=	150ml
¾ cup	=	185ml
1 cup	=	250ml
1¼ cups	=	300ml
1½ cups	=	375ml
1⅔ cups	=	400ml
1¾ cups	=	450ml
2 cups	=	500ml
2½ cups	=	600ml
3 cups	=	750ml
3½ cups	=	800ml
4 cups	=	1 liter
5 cups	=	1.2 liters
6 cups	=	1.5 liters
8 cups	=	2 liters

Dry Measures

¼oz	=	10g
½oz	=	15g
¾oz	=	20g
1oz	=	25g
1½oz	=	40g
2oz	=	50g
2½oz	=	65g
3oz	=	75g
3½oz	=	90g
4oz	=	115g
4½oz	=	130g
5oz	=	150g
5½oz	=	165g
6oz	=	175g
6½oz	=	185g
7oz	=	200g
8oz	=	225g
9oz	=	250g
10oz	=	275g
11oz	=	300g
12oz	=	350g
14oz	=	400g

15oz	=	425g
1lb	=	450g
1¼lb	=	500g
1½lb	=	675g
2lb	=	900g
2¼lb	=	1kg
3–3½lb	=	1.5kg
4–4½lb	=	1.75kg
5–5¼lb	=	2.25kg
6lb	=	2.75kg

Butter

1 tbsp	=	15g
2 tbsp	=	25g
3 tbsp	=	45g
4 tbsp	=	55g
5 tbsp	=	75g
6 tbsp	=	90g
⅓ cup	=	75g
½ cup	=	120g
⅔ cup	=	150g
¾ cup	=	175g
1 cup	=	225g
1½ cups	=	350g

Sugar

¼ cup	=	4 tbsp
⅓ cup	=	75g
scant ½ cup	=	100g
½ cup	=	120g
¾ cup	=	175g

scant 1 cup	=	200g
1 cup	=	225g
1¼ cups	=	275g
1½ cups	=	350g
1¾ cups	=	400g
2 cups	=	450g

Confectioners' sugar

¼ cup	=	25g
½ cup	=	55g
1 cup	=	120g
1½ cup	=	175g
1¾ cup	=	225g

Flour

¼ cup	=	25g
½ cup	=	55g
⅔ cup	=	75g
¾ cup	=	100g
1 cup	=	120g
1¼ cups	=	145g
1½ cups	=	175g
1¾ cups	=	200g
2 cups	=	225g
2¼ cups	=	250g
2½ cups	=	275g
3 cups	=	350g
3½ cups	=	400g
4 cups	=	450g
4¼ cups	=	500g
6½ cups	=	750g

Index